DRIVING
AND JUDGING
DRESSAGE

DRIVING AND JUDGING DRESSAGE

HRH THE DUKE *of* EDINBURGH

J.A. ALLEN · LONDON

British Library Cataloguing in Publication Data
A catalogue record for this book is available from the
British Library.

ISBN 0.85131.666.2

Published in Great Britain in 1996 by
J. A. Allen & Company Limited
1 Lower Grosvenor Place
London SW1W 0EL

Typeset by Textype Typesetters, Cambridge
Edited by Elizabeth O'Beirne-Ranelagh
Designed by Paul Saunders
Photographs by Alf Baker

Colour processing by Tenon & Polert Colour Scanning, Hong Kong.
Printed in Hong Kong by Dah Hua Printing Press Co.

CONTENTS

— 1 —

INTRODUCTION

THE PURPOSE of this little treatise is to pass on a few lessons learnt by someone who has had a certain measure of experience of driving teams of horses and ponies in national and international combined driving events. However, I freely admit that I have rather less experience of dressage judging. This may limit my qualifications, but if a driver can do fairly well in dressage competitions I suggest it implies that he has some knowledge of how to please the judges. It is written in the hope that it might help newcomers to the sport.

In preparing this book, I sought the opinions and advice of several experienced judges and drivers, but while I have incorporated some of their comments and ideas, it remains a personal point of view. It won't please everyone, but where there is a divergence of view, I believe it is more about emphasis than about matters of principle.

The point of writing for both drivers and judges is that theirs is a symbiotic relationship. Since they have such an influence on each other, it struck me that it might be helpful to discuss their separate problems at the same time. I started competitive driving while I was President of the FEI and at several Championships I drove into the arena and saluted the President of the Jury, who was also Chairman of the FEI Driving Committee. It made for interesting discussions at subsequent Bureau meetings.

Purists in dressage will doubtless be scandalised by the pragmatic approach to the subject. So much that is written about dressage is wonderfully romantic, but hardly serves the purpose of helping people who spend hours trying desperately to get uncomprehending horses to tolerate what must appear to them to be unreasonable demands to perform odd manoeuvres in a rectangular arena.

When the Bureau of the FEI was considering the introduction of international rules for carriage driving events, it decided to base the

Whatever the horses may be doing individually and however tense the situation may be for George Bowman, this is a picture of real 'togetherness' and is an illustration of the art of driving a four-in-hand.

competition on the ridden three-day event which, of course, includes a dressage test. The French word 'dressage' is usually translated to mean 'training', but it could also be taken to mean 'deportment' and the test for riders is designed to assess the level or elegance of the deportment of horse and rider while performing a series of movements at various paces. It is worth bearing in mind that, both for the ridden three-day event and the combined driving event, the dressage test is only one part and its value is rated at 3, compared to 12 for the marathon and 1 for the cones competitions. The ridden dressage test for the three-day event is itself somewhat remote from classical or 'Grand Prix' dressage, and the driven test is even further removed from both.

By choosing to adopt the term 'dressage' for the first competition in the driving event, the FEI unwittingly implied that there was some sort of affinity between ridden and driven dressage. Horses may be involved in both disciplines, but the demands and the solutions could hardly be more different. Since there is no driving equivalent to Grand Prix dressage, it might have been better, or more accurate, to have described the dressage tests for combined driving events as 'Compulsory Figures', for that is what it is all about.

It should be very apparent that what you can make a horse do while sitting on a saddle on its back is not the same as what you can persuade it to do while sitting on a carriage behind one horse, let alone behind a pair, a tandem or a team of four. Furthermore, a turnout of a team of four horses can have an overall length of some 10 m. It is also unreasonable to expect a horse to maintain exactly the same outline with the weight of a rider on its back and when it is pulling even the lightest carriage behind it.

There is no doubt that the development of the paces and carriage of any horse can only be achieved while riding. For one thing, a rider is in much closer contact with the horse and has the advantage of being able to use legs, spurs and whip as aids both during training and in the course of a test. Needless to say, most of the training of driving horses is done under saddle before going on to work in harness.

When the horse is in harness, some of these so-called 'aids', like legs and spurs and double bridles, cannot be used at all, although it is, of course, possible to make a driving bit more severe by dropping the reins from the 'cheek' to the 'bar'. Neither the reins nor the whip can be applied to a

Various driving bits: LEFT *(from top) four-ring Wilson snaffle; Army reversible (elbow) bit; Buxton coaching bit.* RIGHT *(from top) Liverpool bit with fixed cheeks; Liverpool bit with turn cheeks, twisted one side bar mouth; Liverpool coaching bit with twisted cheeks.*

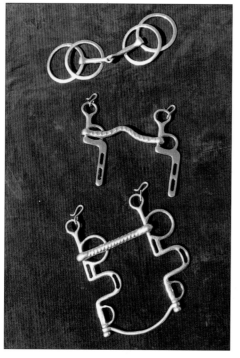 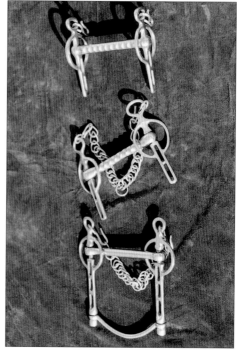

Competing at Lowther in 1996, 23 years after my first competition, but this time in early August and in much better weather conditions.

driven horse in exactly the same way. Leaders' reins can be up to eight yards long. Furthermore, in pairs and teams, the inside, or coupling reins, have to cross over to the inside of the bits on the other horse, so that the pull on the inside of the bit is more to one side, rather than directly back to the driver's hands. It is difficult enough to touch a single horse with a whip in the chosen place; it becomes virtually impossible with a tandem or a team. The only aid enjoyed by a driver, but seriously discouraged in a rider, is the discreet use of the voice, although it has its limitations. If it is used too often and too loudly, it does not make a good impression on judges or spectators.

The first dressage test I ever drove at a competition was at the first Lowther Castle event in 1973. At that time it was held early in May. I was first to go in and there was snow still on the ground. Because of the wet conditions at Windsor that spring, I had been practising on the cinder arena, built for the King's Troop while its barracks in St John's Wood were being re-furbished. The horses had got used to this hard going and were not at all impressed by the sticky going at Lowther as the snow melted. I must have been quite vocal in my efforts to get them moving because a comment by the judge at C read 'too much voice'.

In ridden dressage it should be possible to ride a complete test without moving the position of the hands on the reins. This might just be possible with a single driven horse and perhaps with a pair, but it is quite impossible with a tandem or a team. This immediately gives a new meaning to such terms as 'behind the bit', 'above the bit', 'on the bit', 'impulsion' and 'contact'. These terms still apply, but the essential element in driving is that the carriage should be pulled by the traces and not by the reins. If the reins are taut, the traces will almost certainly be slack. Leaders are not expected to do more than 'carry' their traces throughout the test, but, if they ever do rather more work in the straights, it is vital that they come out of draft in corners, so that they do not pull the pole across before the wheelers have reached the corner. Indeed, many experienced leaders automatically drop out of draft when they start a corner. This means that they have to be lighter in hand than the wheelers and this can sometimes make it look as if they have lost impulsion.

Needless to say, lightness in hand does not mean that the leader reins, or the traces, should be hanging in loops. Unless the driver is in contact with their mouths at all times, it becomes impossible to steer the leaders.

Accuracy of figures is absolutely vital in a dressage test and that means getting close to the boards and turning at the correct points.

This is particularly the case in any single-handed movement; something, incidentally, that riders are rarely expected to attempt.

The fact is that, during a test, the driven horse, or horses, have to do the paces, use the appropriate muscles and maintain the desired 'shape' and head carriage all of their own free will. They will only do this if they have been properly and sympathetically trained under saddle.

The clue to a good driving horse is its lightness in hand, its response to the voice and to the signals coming from the reins. Even with the brakes full on, a team or tandem driver cannot significantly increase the pressure on the bits. In effect, he is merely pulling himself and the carriage up to the horses by the reins. Unless he takes to two-handed driving, steering under these circumstances becomes extremely difficult. Pulling wheelers are bad enough, but if the leaders are heavy in hand, with their reins twanging like harp-strings, dressage becomes a disaster. It is against this background that the meaning of the terms 'on the bit' and 'behind the bit' for driven horses needs to be interpreted.

There is one further very important difference between ridden and driven dressage. In ridden dressage there is only one competitor riding one horse, whereas in the driven version there are eight different classes. There are singles, pairs, tandems and teams of horses and of ponies and there are two sizes of arenas. It is self-evident that the drivers of these different turnouts have rather different problems when it comes to driving any given test.

This suggests that I should write something appropriate for each class, but I suspect it would make rather tedious repetitive reading. I have therefore written mostly about teams of horses in the belief that the basic principles apply to all the classes and equally to horses and ponies.

OVERLEAF *The photographs on pages 12, 13, 14 and 15 show the four possible turnouts with either horses or ponies.*

Singles have a lot of work to do, even though the carriage may be quite light. The choice for singles and tandems is whether to use a two-wheeled or a four-wheeled carriage. Two-wheelers are lighter, but they are not so flexible, since the turnout is rigid from the ends of the shafts to the back of the carriage. Unless the weight in the carriage is very carefully balanced, the shafts will either bear down on the horse or lift it off its feet. This is not a problem with a four-wheeler and, since the carriage has a turn-table, the horse has greater freedom of movement. The FEI now requires all singles to be driven to a four-wheeled vehicle during the marathon phase at international competitions.

All classes have a choice between neck-collar and breast-collar harness and whether to use the breeching or not. Breeching certainly helps horses to slow down, stop and rein-back, but, in dressage at least, this is not normally a serious problem and can be achieved by the pole straps or by the attachment of the harness to the shafts in singles and tandems.

A team of four horses driven two-handed by Valere Standaert of Belgium.

A pair of horses driven by Alwyn Holder, who was one of the first to drive a team in FEI competitions.

A single horse driven by James Lewis to a four-wheeled dual purpose vehicle. These are popular as they can be used for all phases of a combined driving competition.

A horse tandem driven to a dual purpose four-wheeled vehicle by René Schoop. Tandems can also be driven to two-wheeled vehicles. The virtue of a four-wheeler is that the shafts are hinged at the splinter bar, so that there is no weight on the wheeler. The vehicle is longer and heavier than a two-wheeler, but it is articulated by a turn-table over the front axle which makes it more flexible.

A team of four ponies driven by Ursula Hirschberg. She was a highly successful pony tandem driver before taking to a four-in-hand.

A pair of ponies driven by Trevor Kimber to a 'traditional' vehicle used only for the dressage and cones competitions.

A single pony driven by Rachel Wood to a two-wheel vehicle. The virtue of a two-wheeler is that it is lighter, but, as the shafts are fixed to the carriage, the weight of the driver and groom has to be very carefully balanced to ensure that there is no upward or downward pressure on the pony. A two-wheeler is, of course, rigid from the ends of the shafts to the wheels.

A pony tandem driven by the Earl of Onslow with his two distinctive palomino ponies.

2

THE ARENA

Before discussing the problems of driving and judging a dressage test, I think it might be worthwhile to consider where the test is to be performed. Appendices B and Ba of the FEI (International Equestrian Federation) Rules for International Carriage Driving Events (1993 Edition) and Appendix B of the British National Rules (1992 Edition) show the size and lettering for standard arenas of 100 m by 40 m and small arenas of 80 m by 40 m. Appendix Ca of the FEI Rules gives the details for two FEI tests for small arenas (although the test sheets do not specify the size of the arena). They are No. 1 (Light) and No. 2 (Medium). The same Appendix gives the details for three tests for standard arenas, namely No. 3 (Advanced), No. 4 (Alternative Advanced) and No. 5. All these tests are also given in Appendix Ca of the British National Rules. In addition, they give the details of four National Tests: No. 4 Advanced, No. 5 Novice and No. 7 Novice (in a standard arena for horse teams, tandems and pairs, and in a small arena for singles and pony pairs).

The larger arena is normally used for teams and tandems, and sometimes for pairs; while the smaller arena is for singles and sometimes for pairs. The diagrams show how the arenas are marked by letters at various points around the perimeter. These are the letters used in the instructions for the test to indicate where each movement starts and ends.

The layout and marking of the arena is very important for both drivers and judges. Drivers need to know where they are required to stop on the centre line at X and at G and it helps to have a mark at D. The judges also need to be able to see these marks, so they should be conspicuous and it may be necessary to renew them every so often.

The letters round the arena cannot always be placed right up against the boards. The snag is that if they are placed some distance away from the boards, they do not provide an accurate aiming mark for drivers, particularly in any diagonal movement across the arena. In such an eventuality, it

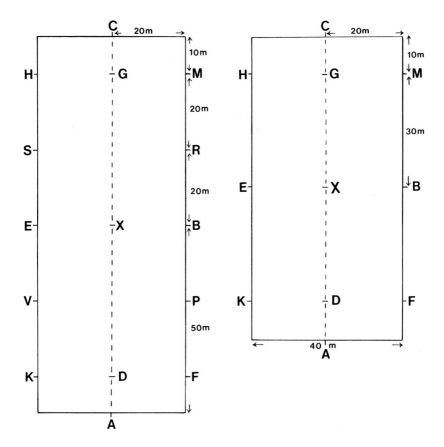

The marking and dimensions of a full-sized 100 m x 40 m arena (LEFT), and (RIGHT) the smaller 80 m x 40 m arena used for singles and sometimes for pairs of ponies.

is a good idea to mark the exact position where the letter should be by a plain white peg as close to the boards as possible.

If there is no convenient reference point, some movements, such as the deviation required in the FEI No. 5 Advanced Test in movements 2 and 4, are difficult both to drive and to judge. Pegs at 10 m either side of A and C would be helpful.

In whichever way the arena is marked, before competing, or taking up their judging positions, it is well worthwhile for both drivers and judges to inspect the arena and its surroundings so as to establish the positions of the letters and marks in relation to the boards and any obvious features in the immediate vicinity, including things that are likely to cause the horses to shy. Some arenas have continuous boarding around them, others have boards placed at intervals. In the latter case, it is very helpful for the

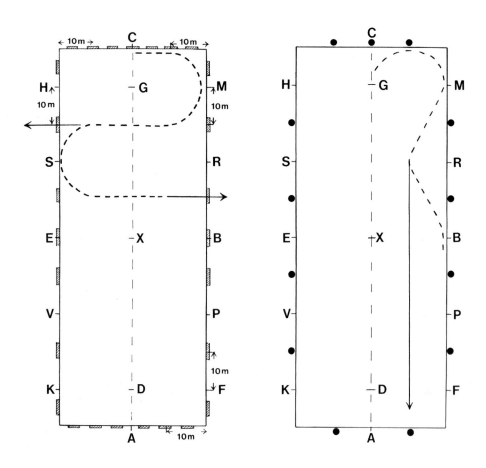

If the boards are not placed end to end around the arena, it helps both drivers and judges if they are placed in such a way as to provide 'aiming marks' and turning points. (LEFT) Boards placed half-way between the letters and 10 m in from the side boards at the ends of the arena. (RIGHT) Where boards are placed end to end, it helps if markers such as pot plants are placed at strategic points, but preferably not too close to the boards.

boards to be sited so that they mark useful points around the arena. For instance, boards placed 10 m either side of A and C and halfway between the letters along the sides are a great help to both drivers and judges.

At many major events, arenas are decorated with pot plants at various points around the boards. Horses almost invariably take exception to these things if they are placed too close to the boards, but it is also important to ensure that they do not obscure any of the letters or markers from the view of judges or drivers. On the other hand, if they are placed in appropriate positions – such as half-way between the markers down the sides of the arena – these decorations can help to provide useful reference points.

Potted plants can help to identify useful 'aiming' points for drivers, but they can also distract the horses. Geoff Woods and his team of horses.

— 3 —

THE RULES

THERE is a well-known, and perceptive, saying: 'When all else fails, read the instructions.' To save you the bother of looking up the FEI and the British National Rules for Competition A, they are printed below. The significant words are printed in italics and paragraphs not directly relevant have been omitted. I have added some comments by way of explanation and in the hope that they may clarify some of the more obscure language.

Article 920 – General and Principles

1. The object of the Dressage Test is to judge the freedom, *regularity of paces*, harmony, *impulsion*, suppleness, *lightness, ease of movement and correct positioning of the horses on the move.*

The competitor will also be judged on his style, accuracy and general command of his team, and on the presentation of the turnout.

2. The *horses will be judged as a team* and not as individual horses, and the *definition of paces* [see below] *will apply to all types of animals.*

Comment These Rules are written for teams of horses – I know of no other types of animals likely to be made to do dressage! – but the principles apply equally to singles, tandems and pairs of horses and ponies.

3. [Not relevant].

4. In combined Driving Events the *Dressage Test must be driven from memory.* No passengers are permitted and the grooms must sit in their correct places.

5. The competitor, when driving the Dressage Test, will *make the change of movement at the time the leaders reach the point indicated on the test.* [British National Rules add the following: *'Circles and half circles which require crossing X or the centre line should be driven in such a manner that the centre line is between the wheels of the carriage,* i.e., either in line with the pole or with the centre of the shafts (in the case of single or tandem).']

Comment The first difficulty is that the whole dressage system was devised for ridden horses, which can follow a track very close to the boards. A carriage, on the other hand, covers more than a metre between its wheels and only the outer wheels can get anywhere near the boards. A single horse can, therefore, only get within a metre of the boards, while only the outside horse in a pair or team can get near the boards.

The point is that, while it is possible to drive the centre of a carriage along the centre line of the arena, it is not possible to get the centre of a carriage closer than about a metre to the boards. This means, in effect, that a half-circle from the centre line to the boards has to be slightly lop-sided. The actual distance from the centre line to the boards may be 20 m, but a carriage can only describe an arc with a 19 m diameter.

The Rule that requires the change of movement to be made 'at the

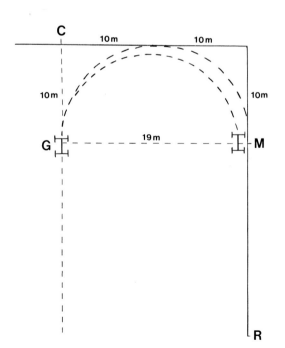

The centre of the carriage can be driven over the centre line of the arena, but it has to be at least one metre from the side boards. This means that the semi-circle between G and M is slightly lop-sided. The problem also arises when driving 20 m circles from X or G.

time the leaders reach the point indicated on the test' needs to be taken as a general one since it cannot be applied precisely in all cases. If it were to be taken literally it would mean, for example, that the 'serpentine' of three or five loops would become more like a zig-zag with drivers attempting to go straight from one 'point indicated' to the next. In practice, drivers are expected to drive even half-circles of 10 m radius (20 m diameter) so that the middle of each half-circle passes close to each 'point indicated' and to drive across the arena exactly half-way between the last and the next 'points indicated'.

It is a different matter when turning on to or off the centre line, since it is the middle of the carriage that should pass over the designated point on the centre line.

Furthermore, while it is reasonable to expect a ridden horse to start and end a movement at exactly the right point, it is extremely difficult, though not impossible – if the movement requires a turn to be started as the leaders reach the appropriate letter by the boards – to get two leaders, two wheelers and the two outside wheels all to pass the desired point in succession.

Some tests contain instructions that are virtually impossible to follow. For example, under movement 1 in the FEI No. 5 Advanced Test, the driver is required to track to the right at C. It is plainly impossible to get the heads of the leaders anywhere near C from the centre line without going out of the arena. It therefore raises the problems of when to start the turn from C to M in movement 1. Strict observance of the Rule means starting the turn as the leaders reach the mark, but it is patently not possible to wait till the horses' heads reach C, so the turn needs to be started between G and C. Since M is given as the point at which the movement ends, it might be assumed that this is the point where the leader should turn on to the side boards. In order to make the best use of the arena, the leaders should turn away from the back line so as to reach the boards at M. That means starting the quarter-circle about 10 m from the corner. If the turn from the centre line is delayed much beyond G, the movement becomes lop-sided. The whole movement looks better if it is made as a smooth half-circle of 19 m diameter starting at G and finishing at M.

A slightly different problem arises in movement 6 in the FEI No. 5 Advanced Test when an extension is required on reaching M followed by a turn at R to go diagonally across the arena to V and passing over X. In order to follow a straight line (RXV) from one side to the other and passing over X, the leaders need to be turned when V is exactly in line with X. If the turn from the boards at R is made at any other point, the driver would either miss X or he would have to put in a 'kink' at X in order to make the turn back on to the boards at V at about the right point.

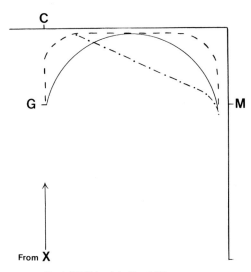

The solid line describes a regular semi-circle between G and M, passing close to the end boards 10 m from the corner. The dashed line illustrates 'going deep into the corners', and the interrupted line shows what might happen if the instructions in the test are followed literally. Each case shows that it is impossible to get near C, the point at which the movement is supposed to begin.

No. 1 'XCM track to the right'

———————— 10 m (approx.) radius half circle
– – – – close as possible to C and corner
–·—·—· direct route C to M

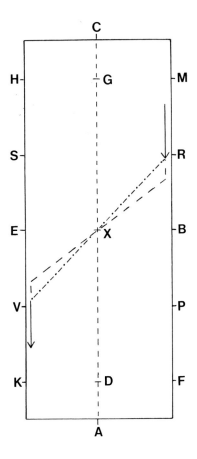

The problem in driving a straight line from R to V and passing over X is that if you start the turn before R, you end up beyond V, and if you start beyond R, you end up short of V.

6. At the halt, the horses must *stand attentive, motionless and straight*, with the weight evenly distributed over all four legs, and be ready to move off at the slightest indication of the competitor.

Comment There appears to be some disagreement among judges about the position of the leaders at a halt. The first part of the leaders to reach the 'point indicated on the test' is their heads, so this implies that their heads should be over the mark. However, this is very difficult for a team driver to judge accurately from his position several metres behind the leaders. It is no easier for the judges when the halt is at X. The practical solution for both drivers and judges is to halt the team with the front feet of the leaders just short of what should be a clearly visible mark.

The transition to the halt should be smooth and precise, with no shuffling. Stopping at exactly the right place is a matter of accuracy.

7. Walk: a free, regular and unconstrained walk of moderate extension is required. The horses must walk *energetically but calmly*, with even and determined steps.

Comment The horses must always walk in a straight line with an even pace and without any of the team breaking into a trot. The problem for judges is to decide how to mark one of a team trotting all the time against the whole team trotting for part of the time.

8. The following trots are recognised: working, collected and extended.

8.1 Working trot – *This is a pace between the extended and the collected trot* and more round than the extended trot. The horses go forward freely and straight, engaging the hind legs with good hock action, on a *taut but light rein*, the position being *balanced* and unconstrained. The steps should be as even as possible. The hind feet touch the ground in the footprints of the fore feet.

The degree of energy and impulsion displayed at the working trot clearly denotes the degree of suppleness and *balance* of the horses.

Comment The length of the reins between the driver's hands and the bits of the leaders is several metres, so that even if the reins do not look taut, there is quite a lot of weight on the bits. As the leaders come out of draft in the corners, their reins are bound to go a bit slacker.

RIGHT *Walking is nothing like as easy as it sounds (as Anna Grayston's expression confirms), particularly with pairs, tandems and teams. There is a lot of luck involved in getting a pair, a tandem or a team to walk together at the same speed and with the same impulsion throughout the movement.*

BELOW *The working trot (shown here by Richard Margrave's team) needs to be that much more lively than the collected trot and, although the horses can be more relaxed, they need to show a greater sense of purpose.*

Note the words 'balanced' and 'balance'. Only a horse in balance can maintain an even rhythm in its paces.

8.2 Collected trot – The neck is raised, thus enabling the shoulders to move with greater ease in all directions, the hocks being well engaged and *maintaining energetic impulsion, notwithstanding the slower movement. The horses' steps are shorter* but they are lighter and more mobile.

8.3 Extended trot – The horses cover as much ground as possible. They *lengthen their stride, remaining on the bit with light contact.* The *neck is extended* and as a result of great impulsion from the quarters, the horses use their shoulders, *covering more ground at each step without their action becoming higher.*

Comment Achieving changes of pace that are immediately apparent to the Judges is the essential requirement, but it is not all that simple. One of the reasons is that the Rules imply – even if they do not put it in so many words – that the difference should be in the length of stride, and not in the rate at which the feet strike the ground nor any increase in the height of the action. However, it is not easy to achieve a noticeable increase in speed without increasing the rate at which the feet strike the ground. If it proves difficult to judge the difference in the length of stride when the feet are striking the ground at the same rate, it is usually possible to notice a difference in the speed of the wheels going around. Note also 'the neck is extended'. This implies that the necks should not be quite so bent as in the other trots.

In practice, the solution for the driver is to make the collected trot as slow as reasonably possible and the extended trot as fast as possible while the horses remain on the bit. The working trot, as the Rules describe it, is somewhere in between. It is worth bearing in mind that, for a big team in an arena of such limited size, it is really only possible for the horses to extend along a straight line. Test No. 5 makes it difficult by expecting a team to extend as it comes out of a corner and just before turning diagonally across the arena. To attempt any corner at an extended trot is bound to affect the balance and rhythm and hence the length of stride, particularly as the outside leader has to go faster to keep in line with the inside horse.

OPPOSITE ABOVE *Christine Dick demonstrates that the collected trot needs special concentration by driver and horses, and success depends on an exact sharing of the work by the horses.*

OPPOSITE BELOW *In effect 'extended' means that the horses need to cover as much ground as possible with each stride. George Bowman's team illustrates this point very clearly.*

9. The rein back is a *kind of walk backwards*. The legs being raised and set down simultaneously by diagonal pairs, the hind legs remaining well in line, and the legs being well raised.

Comment The one thing about the rein-back that causes most comment is whether the whole turnout remains straight. This is largely a matter of luck, but four things are equally, if not more, important about the halt and rein-back. (a) The transition to the halt, (b) standing still for 10 seconds, (c) moving the whole team back straight together for three metres quietly and calmly without any signs of resistance, and (d) the transition to walking forward.

The halt can be improved by using the brakes gently for the last couple of paces and then releasing them as the wheelers come to a stop.

Chester Weber of the United States demonstrates a calm, straight and unresisting rein-back.

This takes the tension off the traces at the last moment. The wheelers are then less likely to want to step back to ease the pressure on their collars, and it also positions them better for the rein-back.

Getting both the carriage and the team to move back straight depends, first, on getting both wheelers to stop together with the carriage straight and on the centre line, secondly, on preventing the horses from anticipating, and thirdly, on getting the wheelers to set off backwards together. Both voice and reins are needed; the voice should be used slowly and quietly and the reins applied gradually. Anything sudden is more likely to send them forward, or to make one or the other throw its head up and jump back. It is more important for the team, as a whole, to move back calmly and without resistance than for the carriage to remain straight.

10. Transitions: *changes of pace and speed must always be made quickly, smoothly and not abruptly.* The cadence of a pace should be maintained up to the moment when the pace is changed or the horses halt. The horses remain light in hand, calm and maintained in a correct position.

Comment Of all the elements in the movements of any test, it is the transitions that are judged most frequently. It is vitally important for all the horses to make the change at the same time and at the right point. An 'abrupt' change of pace occurs when one or several horses either jump forward into their collars, or when the leaders drop back on to the bars. In changing up a pace it is essential for the leaders to move forward at the same time as the wheelers, otherwise the wheelers will catch up the leaders and this will ruin the transition. Dropping down a pace can be helped by a judicious touch on the brakes to prevent the carriage running on to the wheelers as they slow down. If ever the brakes are used, they should not be applied with sufficient force to lock the wheels. Locked wheels do not impress the judges.

11. Presentation: *the appearance of the driver and grooms, the cleanliness, fit, match and condition of the harness, horses, and vehicle will be judged.*

Comment It may sound obvious, but drivers and grooms always look better when they sit up straight and are appropriately and neatly dressed. The FEI produced a little booklet on the subject of dress some years ago. In principle, it is the type of carriage and harness in use that decides what the appropriate dress should be.

The method of judging Presentation is laid down in the next Article:

Article 921 – Method of Judging

1. The Judges will allocate their marks individually and there will be *no consultation among Judges once the Competition has commenced…*

2. *Presentation will be judged by the Ground Jury as an item of General Impression, marked while the Dressage Test is being driven.*

Comment Judging cleanliness and condition of the harness and horses, while trying at the same time to judge the test itself, is quite a task. It is easy enough to form a general impression. What catches the eye is the sparkle of the brass or chrome fittings and the shine on the carriage and horses. The 'match' of the horses has as much to do with the similarity of their paces and head carriage as it does with their size and colour.

Properly fitted bridles, blinkers and Liverpool bits.

The problem is to remember to judge 'Presentation' while the driver is in the arena. It is a good idea to get the writer to remind the judge to do so at a convenient moment during the test, otherwise it is inclined to be left till the drivers have completed their tests and left the arena. In Test No. 5, the 'serpentine' provides a reasonable opportunity for this purpose. It is also a good idea to judge the fit of the harness methodically by starting with the bridles and working back towards the carriage.

The first thing to notice is the fit of the blinkers. The middle of the blinkers should be opposite the eyes and neither so 'shut' that the horse is unable to see anything, nor so wide open that they flap about. The nose-band on the bridle should be between the eyes and the nostrils and not too tight. The throat lash should only be tight enough to prevent the bridle from being pulled off the horse's head. If it is too tight, it will prevent the horse from holding its head properly; that is to say, with the front of its head about vertical to the ground. The bit should be close to,

OPPOSITE *In the original FEI Rules, 'Presentation' was judged at the halt before the dressage test itself. Mary Matthews driving a pair.*

but not pressing on the sides of the mouth, with the curb chain loose enough only to be effective when considerable pressure is exerted by the reins on the bit. It is worth noting the size of the bits and where the reins are connected to them. The ease or severity of the bit tells its own story.

Breast collars should not be so high as to press on the wind-pipe and not so low that they interfere with the leg action. Neck collars should fit exactly. The pole end should be roughly at the same height as the breast collars or opposite the bottom of a neck collar, so that it does not pull down on the pole-straps or lift them up. The fit of the breeching, traces and pole-straps is interrelated; neither so tight that they constrain the movements of the horse, nor so loose that they flop about.

The neck collar harness is said to be the most efficient way of transferring the energy of the horse to the carriage. Its only disadvantage is that each collar needs to be individually fitted and the whole harness is somewhat heavier than the breast collar harness. Team of horses driven by Richard Oddie.

The breast collar harness is lighter and a good deal easier to put on and take off than the neck collar. It is simple to adjust to individual horses and this is most important, because the collar must not be so high that it presses on the wind-pipe or so low that it interferes with the working of the horse's shoulders. Pivoted bars on the splinter bar, to take the wheelers' traces, are essential with breast collar harness, otherwise their shoulders will be rubbed raw in a very short time. Sheryl Leibowitz of the Republic of South Africa with her pony pair.

The back-pad needs to be central and just behind the withers and just tight enough to keep it in position. The fit of the crupper is really important. Too loose and it will not help to keep the back-pad in the right place; too tight and it will cause the horse great discomfort and may easily rub the skin at the top of the dock.

The crupper needs to be fitted with great care and the traces and breeching (when used) must be precisely adjusted.

3. [Not relevant.]

4. [Not relevant.]

5. In case of *marked lameness, the President of the Jury informs the competitor that he is eliminated. There can be no appeal against this decision.*

Comment This decision is the responsibility of the judge at C alone. The chances of a driver coming into the arena with a horse that is markedly lame are fairly remote. A more frequent, and more difficult, situation arises when there is a suspicion of lameness. If the judge at C decides to stop the driver and it subsequently turns out that the horse was not lame, the driver has no chance to repeat the test. When there is a suspicion of lameness, the judge at C would be well advised to tell the driver at the end of the test that he is going to instruct the Veterinary Official to check the horse immediately.

Article 923 – Scoring

1. Points will be awarded for each numbered movement and for each heading under the General Impression, on the following basis:

10	Excellent	5	Sufficient
9	Very good	4	Insufficient
8	Good	3	Fairly bad
7	Fairly good	2	Bad
6	Satisfactory	1	Very bad
0	Not executed		

Comment To be fair to a driver, judges should only judge the factors mentioned in the test sheet for each movement. A persistent characteristic that does not directly affect the accuracy of the test – head shaking, tail swishing, hanging back etc. – is better marked under the General Impression headings at the bottom of the score sheet. These are common to all tests and are shown in Appendix Ca of the FEI Rules.

Each test consists of eleven movements and five headings under General Impression, so that the latter amount to one third of the total marks available. This should be ample to mark down undesirable characteristics.

The General Impressions are numbered from 12 to 16:

12.	Paces	Regularity and freedom (if equipe [teams], maintenance of pace by all horses)
13.	Impulsion	Moving forward with elasticity of steps, relaxation of the back, and engagement (if equipe, all horses working).
14.	Obedience and lightness	Response to aids, willing and without resistance.
15.	Driver	Use of aids; handling of reins and whip, position on box, accuracy of figures
16.	Presentation	Appearance of driver and grooms; cleanliness, fitness, matching and condition of horses, harness and vehicle.

For comments on 'General Impressions', see Chapter 5 below.

2. [Refers to Articles about dress and whip, vehicles and harness.]

3. Should a competitor make an *error of course*, the President of the Jury or his representative *will ring the bell and stop the competitor, who must then continue the Test from the point where the error was made.* Should *harness become disconnected or broken, the President of the Jury must ring the bell, and a groom must dismount to make the repair.*

For an *error of course or if a groom dismounts* (for any reason), penalties will be attributed as follows:

First incident	5 penalties	Third incident	15 penalties
Second incident	10 penalties	Fourth incident	Elimination

Comment Penalties for an 'Error of Course' are *only awarded by the judge at C.* Since there is no time penalty, drivers who have been stopped for making an error of course should always drive up to the judge at C and ask for clarification, even if they appreciate where they have gone wrong, so as to be certain at which point the judge wishes them to resume the test. If a driver attempts to continue before speaking to the judge, the judge at C should ring the bell again and call the driver over to explain what has happened and what he wants the driver to do next.

Going wrong in a test is the dread of all novices, but it can also happen to experienced drivers. It is most likely to happen if the driver is having a problem with one or all the horses or is distracted for some other reason. I once managed to get the loop of my whip over my head just as I was starting the serpentine. By the time I had got it off again I had lost count of the number of loops I had made and succeeded in doing one extra. In those days there was a time limit, so I was penalised for the error and had time faults as well. Without them, I should have won the whole event.

A general problem for the judge at C is to decide the difference between 'Not Executed', which carries a score of 0 from each of the judges, and an 'Error of Course', which requires him to ring the bell to indicate that the driver should go back and do the correct movement, and to give the driver 5 penalty points. By implication, the difference is that 'Not Executed' refers to a movement in which the driver has been unable to get his horses to do the required pace; for example, where most of a team trots throughout the movement intended to be at a walk, or when most of the team canters throughout a movement intended to be at an extended trot. It could also apply in a case where the driver has obviously made an attempt, but has only managed a circle that hardly comes within a reasonable description of such a shape.

It would seem, therefore, that 'Error of Course' applies to cases where the team is under complete control, but where the driver loses his memory and executes a movement which should be driven at a different point of the test, or which is no part of the test at all.

A marginal case is where a driver forgets to halt or change direction or pace at the right point, but then remembers some distance further on and carries out the required change before the judge at C has decided that the driver has committed an 'Error of Course'. In principle, the judge should ring the bell as soon as a driver has, significantly, passed the point where a movement should begin. If the driver remembers before the judge rings the bell, he should be marked down appropriately by all the judges.

However, there will always be awkward cases; for instance, where a deviation is required, and a driver only begins to move away from the side boards beyond the appropriate mark, or overshoots the mark for a halt. The judge only has a very short time to decide whether the movement was 'Not Executed' or whether it was an 'Error of Course' and ring the bell. If he lets it go, all the other Judges have to decide whether it was '0 – Not Executed' or whether it was anything from '4 – Insufficient' to '1 – Very Bad'.

The consequences for the score of the driver are quite interesting. Say a driver is doing reasonably well till he has a lapse of memory. He is then stopped by the bell and made to do the movement again. At his second attempt he is given 7 marks by each judge, so that he gets 3 penalty points in his final score, but he is also given 5 penalty points from the judge at C. The net result is 8 penalty points for that movement. On the other hand, if the judge at C decided that it was not an 'Error of Course', in order for the driver to be given the same number of penalty points all the judges would have to mark it as 'Bad' and give him 2 marks each. It would need all the judges to decide that the movement had not been executed at all to have the effect of giving him 10 penalties for that movement in his final score.

This Rule also specifies that a groom must dismount and correct any failure of equipment and that this incurs 5 penalties. If the judge rings the bell, to stop the driver for failure of equipment, while the driver is on the course, the penalty is 5 points and the driver should continue from where he stopped. Should the driver make an error of course as a result of a failure of equipment, the judge should ring the bell and call the driver over to him as soon as the repair has been made and instruct the driver where to resume the test. In this case the problem is to decide whether these are a first and second incident and, therefore, whether the driver should be given 5 penalties for an error of course – as the first incident – and then 10 for putting a groom down – as the second incident, making a total of 15; or whether the driver incurs 5 penalties for putting a groom down for the first time and a further 5 for making an error of course for the first time, making a total of 10. It all depends on the interpretation of Paragraph 3. The words 'For an error of course OR if a groom dismounts' suggest that they should be treated as separate incidents and given 5 penalties each.

4. *Leaving the arena* in any way other than as is laid down for the Test is grounds for a *disciplinary offence.* If the *whole turnout leaves the Dressage arena during the test the penalty must be elimination.* If only part of the turnout leaves the arena the competitor should be *marked down for inaccuracy of the movement.*

Comment The first sentence seems to have been a victim of translation from French to English. An unauthorised action can only be grounds for a penalty. In this case, as in many others in a driving event, the penalty is elimination.

The decision to eliminate a driver is the sole responsibility of the judge at C. Marking down for inaccuracy should be done by each judge. The decision about what marks to give obviously depends on the circumstances. Just kicking a board, or putting a foot outside the arena where there is a gap in the boards, is always likely to happen if a driver tries to get as close to the boards as possible, and should not warrant the deduction of more than one mark – if that.

If it appears that the driver has temporarily lost control, or one of his horses is simply playing up, there is a case for treating the movement as 'Bad' or 'Very Bad' and marking accordingly.

5. Dressage Tests are not timed. The Test begins as the team enters the arena and *ends as the team moves off after the second salute.* The time shown on the judging sheets is for scheduling information only. The competitor must start his Dressage Test within 90 seconds from the sound of the bell, otherwise he will be eliminated.

Comment In all FEI tests, the instruction to 'Leave the arena at a (working) trot' comes under the last scored movement. However, the instruction appears, and the movement takes place, after the final salute. This implies that the test is concluded before the driver sets off to leave the arena. Consequently, only a gross disregard for the instruction would warrant marking down, perhaps under 'Driver'.

6. The total points awarded by each Judge will be added together and divided by the number of judges. Any penalties under Article 923.3, awarded by the Judge at C, will be deducted from the total. The *competitor with the highest total will be placed first* in Competition A. In a Combined Driving Event, the total points will then be *rounded to the nearest whole number and deducted from the maximum* allowed for the Test to become penalty points.

Comment Only the judge at C can award penalties. 'The highest total' and 'the maximum allowed' refer to the good marks awarded by the judges.

'Rounded to the nearest whole number' is not explained, but it is taken to mean that scores with – 0.5 and above move to the next higher whole number, while – 0.4 and below move to the lower whole number.

4

MOVEMENTS

EVERY TEST of whatever level demands the execution of seven basic 'movements': driving along straight lines; quarter, half and full circles (these may be of various diameters, although – by implication – half circles from the centre to the side boards or from the side to the centre line should, theoretically, be of 20 m diameter); minor changes of direction; halts and rein-back. The Rules specify four different paces: three trots – collected, working and extended (or lengthened strides) – and the walk, but they say little about the movements. The judges give marks for these movements, but they also give marks for the transitions from one movement to another.

The very first movement in every test is the entry to the arena at A and then up the centre line to X. This may sound fairly simple, but it is probably the point of greatest anxiety for the driver and it cannot be done properly unless the whole turnout is going straight and at the right pace before it enters the arena. One way of getting prepared for an entry to the arena is by driving a rough 'figure of eight' in the collecting ring so that the turnout is facing and opposite the entry each time it reaches the cross-over point at the middle of the figure.

The second movement is invariably a 'Halt and Salute'. The transition to the halt should be smooth and straight from the trot. In other words, the horses should stop dead just short of the mark without shuffling for the last few steps and remain stationary without stepping back or sideways and preferably without looking around or waving their heads about. As already mentioned, the wheelers can be helped by gently applying the brakes just before the horses come to a stop and then releasing them at the last moment to allow the tension to come off the traces. Provided the leaders are not in draft, there should be no reason for them to step back when they stop.

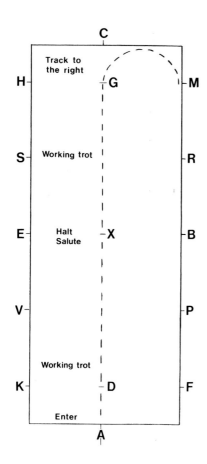

The first movement in Advanced Test No. 5. Note that judges are required to assess six distinct elements and then to give the whole movement a score out of 10.

The 'Salute' should not start until the horses have stopped and it should not be hurried. Gentlemen must first transfer the whip (and the reins, if not already in the left hand) to the left hand and remove the hat by the front of the brim, or by the crown, and raise it slightly forward and above the head, although there is nothing against the continental practice of sweeping the hat down at arm's length beside the carriage. Tipping the hat forward as if expecting a donation does not look very good. Having moved the reins to the left hand, ladies salute with their whip. The traditional way of doing this is by raising it to a horizontal position in front of the eyes. There is no need to bow the head as well. According to Sally Walrond, judges appreciate a smile at the end of a test.

The salute should be deliberate from start to finish and it is most important not to let the horses move until the whip has been transferred back to the right hand, the reins are re-arranged as necessary and the driver is ready to move off. The whole team should then move off together without deviating from the centre line.

*I would say that George Bowman (*TOP*) has got his salute about right, although his horses are not quite settled. Mine is a bit too elaborate (*BELOW*) and I would judge Georgina Frith's (*OPPOSITE ABOVE*) as just a fraction too high.*

The next movement is almost invariably a half-circle from the centre line (some tests require the movement to begin at C, but this is obviously impossible). However, it does imply that the turn need not start exactly at G although, in my opinion, it looks better if the movement is a continuous turn from G to M or H. Since the instruction says that it should end at either M or H it implies that the leaders should not reach the side boards before the appropriate letter. The whole turnout should be as close as possible to the end boards about halfway between C and the side of the arena, and again at the side boards when it reaches M. This is most important as it is all very close to the judge at C and if a 'deviation' or an 'extension' is required from M or H, it works better if the carriage is as close to the boards at M or H as possible.

The important point to remember is that all movements – and that includes turns and circles – should begin when the leaders' heads reach the relevant letter and finish when their heads reach the letter at the end of the movement.

Turning any sort of corner with a team has always been a problem. The difficulty is that the reins to the leaders pass through roger rings attached to the outside of the wheelers' bridles just below their ears. When one or other of the leader reins is pulled and the leaders begin to turn, the rein also tends to pull the inside wheeler's bridle inwards. At the same time the outside leader's rein presses on the outside wheeler's head. Furthermore, if the leaders are exerting any pressure on their traces, it will pull the end of the pole round and make it very difficult for the driver to hold the wheelers away from the corner till they are in the right position to follow the leaders.

In the ordinary course of driving a team, 'holding-off' the wheelers at a corner has usually been done by taking a loop of the leader rein under the left thumb and then holding the outside wheeler rein with the right hand. It is also possible to do it by slipping the outside wheeler rein over the left thumb before reaching the corner. The advantage of this method is that it leaves the right hand free to adjust the inside leader rein to achieve exactly the right rate of turn required.

However, when it comes to dressage, the snag about all this is that holding the wheelers off inevitably turns their heads away from the corner, which is considered to be a bad fault by judges used to ridden dressage. It is for this reason that it is very important for the leaders to be out of draft on going into a corner and not to anticipate the turn, and for the wheelers to be trained not to turn until they get the signal from the driver. A touch of the whip on the inside wheeler, or just calling its name, at the critical moment should be sufficient to keep the wheelers going into the corner.

When turning from the side of the arena on to the centre line, it is absolutely essential for the whole turnout to pass directly over the required point on the centre line. This also applies to any movements diagonally across the arena when the turnout must pass directly over X.

In the ordinary course of events, changing paces means just that and the Rules suggest how it should be achieved. However, there are some points to be borne in mind. If pressed too suddenly, attempts to get a team to change up to an extended trot can often result in the leaders, or one or both wheelers, responding by breaking into a canter. There is also the risk of the wheelers setting off first so that they run up to the leaders.

Turning into an extension and turning during an extension can cause problems if the leaders are not on their bits. The leaders' reins then go slack and for a few critical moments it is very difficult to steer them. The art is to get the whole team to accelerate as quickly as possible without any of the horses feeling like over-doing it. There are further problems if the extension is expected to continue past points P and V and then drop to a working trot at F or K. The kink in the track at P and V unbalances the team and the approach of the corner after K or F does not help to maintain the rhythm across the end of the arena.

At some stage of the more advanced tests, drivers are invited to execute a circle, or a deviation, with the reins held in one hand. It is important for drivers to make sure that the right hand is removed from the reins *before* the leaders reach the mark and is not returned to the reins till the leaders

The art in driving a single-handed circle is to get the leaders to turn before the wheelers so that the whole turnout, including the carriage, follows the circumference of the circle. (TOP) *The author with his team of Fell ponies.* (BELOW) *Christoph Sandmann of Germany.*

have reached the point at the end of the movement. In executing the movement, much depends on the leaders being out of draft, so that the wheelers are not encouraged into cutting the corners. Assuming that the wheelers do not 'drop in' as the circle is performed, and since individual leaders on the inside of the circle are likely to respond differently to the pull on the rein, the driver needs to take an appropriately sized loop in the respective leader rein under the left thumb. The point to remember is exactly how much of a loop is needed for each leader and when to slip the loop to get the team to straighten out after completing the circle.

As the wheelers are also unlikely to respond in exactly the same way, it may be necessary, in the case of a wheeler that is inclined to drop in at a corner, to slip its rein over the left thumb before starting the circle. This sounds fairly easy, but it has to be done quickly just before taking a loop in the leader's rein. After that the shape of the circle can be influenced by treating the reins like the tiller of a boat. Moving the left hand to the left has the effect of shortening the right rein and vice versa.

Some tests require circles or half-circles with diameters of less than 20 m. The problem here, both for drivers and judges, is to estimate the size of the circle within the context of the arena. There is no easy solution to this problem and there are bound to be differences of opinion between drivers and judges. The same applies when a movement requires a 'deviation' of so many metres from a straight line between two letters. This is probably easier for a driver to get right than for a judge to check. The driver can at least see both the centre line and the side boards and the position of the boards at the end of the arena. The judge, or judges, on the other hand, are looking at the turnout from an angle.

All tests include three halts and a rein-back. I have discussed these movements under their respective Rules.

Dressage tests may look fairly slow-moving affairs, but it is surprising how much rein handling takes place, and if a rein slips or becomes misplaced for some reason – some wheelers are adept at 'stealing' a bit of their rein and one leader may be heavier in hand than the other – there is little opportunity to get it back into the right position. One helpful indication is the relative position of the buckles of the connecting reins. If they are opposite each other, the reins are about equal (provided the coupling reins are equal in the first place). In order to ensure that the reins always remain in the pre-determined position, there is much to be said for buckling the reins together so that, whatever happens, they always go back to a datum position against the buckle in the palm of the left hand. The principle works equally well with tandems, pairs and singles.

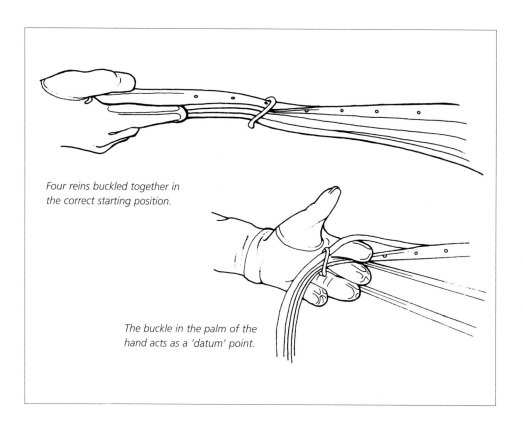

Four reins buckled together in
the correct starting position.

The buckle in the palm of the
hand acts as a 'datum' point.

5

JUDGING

INTERNATIONAL events and championships are judged by five judges. The President sits at C and the other four judges at M, H, F and K. National events are usually judged by three judges. The President sits at C and the others at B and E.

It is usual in Club events, and sometimes in Novice classes, for only one judge at C to mark the tests. This judge can see whether a driver is going straight up the middle line and he can see the deviations, circles and half-circles, but little else. Where there is only one judge, I believe there is a case for placing him in the middle of one side of the arena at either B or E so that he gets a better view of both ends of the arena.

In principle, the purpose of the dressage tests is to examine the ability of the driver and to demonstrate the level of training of the horses. The training for the basic skills demanded by the dressage test – obedience, calmness and lightness in hand – is equally relevant to negotiating the obstacles and getting round the cones course. Without this basic training, a driver would find it difficult to do a reasonable test. It is also extremely unlikely that he would be able to to drive sufficiently accurately to achieve a good score in the marathon or a clear round in the cones.

Article 920 (quoted in full in Chapter 3 above) uses a lot of technical expressions, some of which are not easy to understand and even more difficult for a driver to implement. For example, what is an average competitor in a combined driving event to make of this bit from Article 920, 8.1: 'Working trot – ... more round ... The horses go forward freely ...engaging the hind legs with good hock action'? Or this: 'Collected trot – The neck is raised, thus enabling the shoulders to move with greater ease in all directions, the hocks being well engaged'?

OPPOSITE *Some form of shelter for judges is a necessity. Sitting for hours in the sun or in the rain or in a strong wind makes judging more demanding than necessary.* (TOP) *Royston Carpenter and* (BELOW) *Michael Freund of Germany.*

Whatever judges may want to see in a ridden dressage test, the three most important factors in a driven test, and the things that drivers really should be able to achieve, are (a) accuracy of figures, (b) perceptible differentiation between paces, and (c) the regularity, balance, lightness in hand and the impulsion of the horses. It is worth noting that the word 'accuracy' appears ten times and 'regularity' eleven times under 'Factors to be Judged' in the FEI No. 5 Advanced Test.

The Rules do not specify exactly what is meant by such terms as 'accuracy', 'regularity', 'resistance', 'disobedience', 'evasion' and 'impulsion'. It is not altogether surprising since they are very difficult to define in so many words. I can only give you my own interpretation.

I would suggest that *'accuracy'* means driving straight, stopping precisely and standing straight and still at the halts with the leaders' feet just short of the marks; it means starting a movement at precisely the right point, turning so that the whole turnout goes past the turning points, both at the start and at the end of a movement, and as close to them as possible, or directly over the marks on the centre line. It means describing exact circles and not ovoids.

This is not as easy as it sounds. As I have pointed out, there may be 20 m between the centre line and the boards, but while the carriage can be driven over the centre line, it cannot be driven over the boards. Therefore the distance available for the circle between, say, D and F is at least 1 m less than the apparent 20 m between the centre line and the side boards and also 1 m less beside the boards at the end of the arena. The result is that the circle tends to get 'squeezed' on the axis between D and F and elongated on the axis between the end boards and the open part of the arena. The same effect occurs when circles are driven starting at X, passing B, or E, and returning to X. Only the three middle half-circles of the serpentine can be driven as having a diameter of exactly 20 m. A careful driver will have established 'aiming points' – individual boards or conveniently placed pot plants – at the sides, or ends, of the arena to ensure that circles, or deviations, are of the right size.

In my opinion, *'regularity'* means achieving and maintaining, without breaks, the prescribed paces for each movement; it means getting the team to move as a whole and, particularly, for the leaders to stay together at all times, to do some work along the straights and to come out of draft at the corners; it means that the team shares out the work evenly and the two wheelers do an equal amount of work at all times. It means that the team as a whole maintains the cadence and rhythm of each pace; it means the horses carrying their heads evenly at the same level and it means an absence of fidgeting, head tossing and tail swishing.

One degree worse than fidgeting is *'resistance'*. Resistance is a polite way of saying that the team is pulling the driver's arms out and so making it very difficult, if not impossible, for the driver to do a free, calm and accurate test. It can also mean a reaction against the application of pressure on the bit by throwing up the head. This is particularly likely to happen during the rein-back if it is attempted too suddenly. Under certain circumstances, it could mean an unwillingness to go forward. Drivers sometimes draw attention to this unwillingness by constant demands to 'trot on'. If resistance persists throughout the test and is having a noticeable effect on the accuracy and regularity of all the movements, there is nothing for it but to mark it down in every movement and under General Impressions as well. However, if it is not too serious it should be marked under 'Obedience and Lightness'.

'Disobedience' is more deliberate than 'resistance'. It would include a horse refusing to respond to the reins to turn one way or the other, or turning its head sideways without moving in the required direction, doing the wrong pace, shying at a pot plant or responding to some distraction in the vicinity of the arena. In principle, a 'disobedience' is likely to be momentary and only affects the movement in which it takes place.

'Evasion' might be taken to be a horse's negative reaction to a driver's aids: dropping behind the bit, swishing its tail or putting its ears back every time it is touched by the whip. The general impression is that the horse does not want to do its work freely and happily.

'Impulsion' is probably the most difficult characteristic to define. In many ways it is the exact opposite to 'evasion'. It denotes a positive willingness to get on with the business obediently and responsively. It should not only be applied to a horse's ability to extend; it requires just as much impulsion to maintain a collected trot. The criterion should be that the horse is evidently making the effort. A team that is obviously light in hand and does the movements accurately and without evasion does not lack impulsion simply because it is not 'flashy'.

The Rules imply that all drivers should be judged primarily on their precision and on the impulsion and regularity of their horses, with other factors treated as a bonus, or a disadvantage. Precision by the driver and the lightness and obedience of the horses are the essential requirements in a dressage test, and if these can be achieved, it should be recognised by the judges.

Many people with a limited understanding of the process of judging are inclined to be critical if the marks given by the individual judges to individual competitors vary by more than a small margin. This is not a fair criticism. In the first place, each judge is seeing the test from a different position and may well notice things that the other judges have missed or been unable to see.

In any case, such variation is not particularly important provided the level of marking by each judge is consistent. That is to say, if one of the judges gives higher (or lower) marks than the average, they should be consistently higher (or lower) than the average of the other judges. It matters rather more that the individual competitors are placed in roughly the same order of merit by each of the judges. The ideal result would be for each of the judges to have placed the competitors in the same order of merit, whatever the total score they gave to each individual competitor.

The very first essential for both judges and drivers is to know the test intimately. Some people can doubtless visualise a test simply by reading the test sheet, but many cannot. A good way for both drivers and judges to get to know a test is to draw a series of rectangles in the proportions of the arena, and put the letters round them in their appropriate places. Each movement can then be drawn in a separate rectangle. (Appendix D of both the FEI and the British National Rules shows such diagrams for some of the movements in some of the tests.) Different colours can be used to indicate different paces. There is usually no difficulty about remembering the paces required in the main movements, it is the bits between these movements that are frequently forgotten or ignored.

Drivers will have learnt the test in advance, although it is probably unwise to practice it in its entirety too often, or the horses will get to know the sequence too well and will start to anticipate the next movement.

If judges are able to drive, it is a good idea for them to have driven the test they are to judge, so as to give them an idea of the problems that the drivers will be facing. At some international events, the judges are invited to judge a driver, who is not among the competitors, before the competition starts so that they can agree on their general approach to the task.

The test sheets attempt to lay down under each movement and under 'General Impressions' precisely what is required of the driver and precisely what the judges should be judging. However, in some cases the instructions can be a bit confusing.

Some instructions make it very difficult for judges to know exactly how much weight to give to each of several factors in a particular movement. For example, the first movement in the FEI No. 5 Advanced Test requires the judges to mark (a) driving on a straight line at a working trot, (b) halt and stand on the bit, and (c) transition to working trot. However, the whole movement takes the driver from A to M, including the instruction to track right at C, so that there are two straight stretches each at a working trot; a transition from a working trot to the halt; the halt itself; the salute, and the transition to a working trot again. Movement 5 in this same test poses much the same problem and there are several similar cases in this

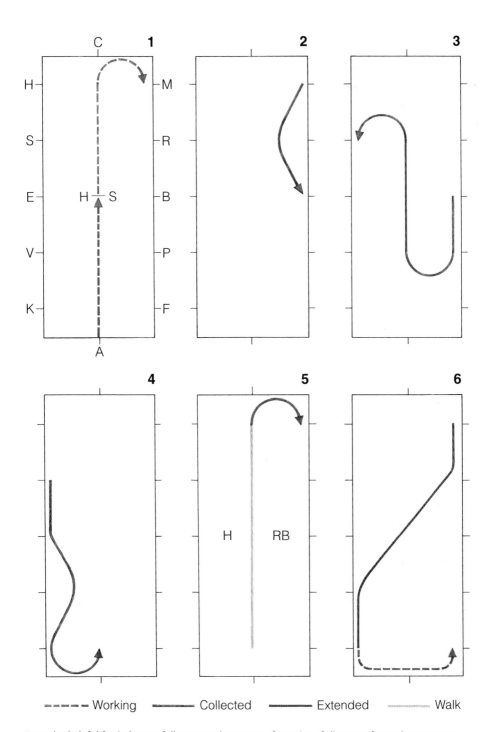

It can be helpful for judges to follow a test by means of a series of diagrams for each movement. These diagrams, and those on page 54, illustrate the movements in No. 5 Advanced Test.

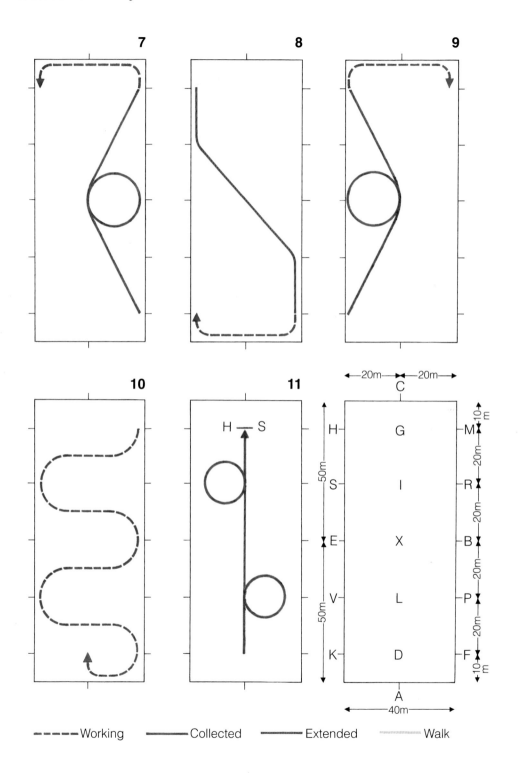

and other tests which do not make life easy for either drivers or judges.

One way of solving this problem of multiple factors in a single movement is to divide the 10 marks roughly equally between the different factors within a movement and mark it accordingly. In other words, as there are six factors in the first movement of FEI No. 5 Advanced Test, counting 0 there are three options available for each (0, 1 or 2). 0 would equal bad, 1 would equal fair and 2 would equal good. One mark for each would therefore come out at 6, which is 'Satisfactory'. If any factor was better than average the mark would go up to 7 or 'Fairly Good'.

It is worth repeating that the dressage test is only one part of a combined driving event. It is of course true that some breeds of horses and ponies look 'smarter' and have better natural paces than others – hackneys and some Welsh ponies, for instance – and this poses quite a dilemma for judges. Just to illustrate the point: if two teams perform the test equally accurately and with equal impulsion and willingness, and the turnout and drivers are equally impressive, should the 'smart' team be given better marks than the other? Should the difference in marks be applied for every movement, or only under General Impression? Opinions vary, but I would suggest that the fair criterion for judging should be the level of training achieved by the horses, whatever their breed, and not the natural conformation and action of the particular breed.

Marking the five factors under General Impressions is probably more difficult than marking the movements themselves. First comes:

12. *Paces.* Regularity and freedom. (If equipe [i.e. team], maintenance of pace by all horses.)

The important point here is that all the horses have maintained the paces required in each movement with an even rhythm and cadence, without any hops and skips or heads waving up and down, and with the leaders keeping together.

13. *Impulsion.* Moving forward with elasticity of steps, relaxation of the back and engagement. (If equipe, all horses working.)

This heading causes most contention, largely because it has to be a matter of subjective judgement. It is very frustrating for a driver to be judged as 'lacking impulsion' when he feels that his team has been light in hand and has done all the movements correctly and accurately and gets reasonably good marks for the movements. However, horses do tend to get bored with dressage, particularly if they have been made to do rather a lot of practice. It is a common experience to have the team going really nicely in the collecting ring and then to have them 'go dead' the moment they enter the arena. They will do the movements all right, but they lack sparkle and the judges see them as unenthusiastic and reluctant to get on with it. When this happens there is nothing that a driver can do about it. I am afraid the contention will continue.

14. *Obedience and lightness.* Response to aids willing and without resistance.

It is usually possible to judge 'lightness' by the tautness of the reins and frequently by the expression on the face of the driver and the tone of his voice! 'Obedience' can be presumed if there has been no evident disobedience.

15. *Driver.* Use of aids; handling of reins and whip, position on box, accuracy of figures.

The driver should be upright on the box, relaxed and steady, elbows close to the sides and managing the reins and whip neatly and without moving the arms more than necessary. Since accuracy is judged under each 'movement', it seems a bit excessive to mark it again. I think the point here is to recognise accuracy generally, ignoring an occasional lapse due to uneven going in the arena or some external distraction, such as a train going past.

16. *Presentation.* Appearance of driver and grooms; cleanliness, fitness, matching, and condition of horses, harness, and vehicle.

This has already been considered under paragraph 11 of Article 920 of the Rules.

There are four columns on a test sheet. They are headed 'Movements', 'To be Judged', 'Marks 0–10' and 'Remarks'. This last one is vitally important for both judges and drivers. Drivers may well accept high marks without bothering too much about the reasons, but they can get very upset by unexplained low marks. The 'Remarks' column is there for judges to note the reasons for their good and bad marks. Many drivers will know full well when they have done something badly, but even so, a judge's view may well help them to do better next time.

However, a certain caution is necessary. During a Club event I put the spare pony – normally a wheeler – in the lead to give it some experience. It did not go well and persistently hung back. The natural consequence was that its rein was often slack, but the other leader succeeded in getting it to do the right movements simply by pushing and pulling. The judge naturally noticed that it was hanging back and that its rein was often slack and must have concluded that I was unable to steer it. The comment under 'Remarks' was that the pony must have known the test!

In many cases, drivers may have simply got into bad habits without noticing. The most common faults are usually due to negligence rather than to lack of training or skill. It should be just as easy to stop in the right as in the wrong place or to get D, X and G exactly between the wheels, or to take the reins in one hand at the right moment. No matter how well the horses are going, if the driver cannot make full use of the arena – in other words, does not drive accurately and close to the boards – marks are simply being thrown away.

The value of the 'Remarks' column for judges is that the comments can serve as a reminder in the event that a driver subsequently seeks an explanation from the judge.

Anyone who judges regularly is bound to get to know what to expect from certain drivers. One of the most difficult problems for judges and their writers is to look at each driver with an entirely fresh and unbiased eye, whatever their previous performances may have been like. Judges may have their preferences for types of horses, but that is usually known to the drivers. Every driver also knows that horses are very unlikely to behave in exactly the same way every time they enter the arena whatever the driver tries to do about it. Judges, and drivers, should always be prepared for major miracles, as well as minor disasters!

At the 1984 World Championships in Hungary at Silvasvarad, I was fortunate enough to get a dressage score of 28 penalty points, with which I was extremely pleased. I was in the lead of the competition until the very last competitor came into the ring. It happened to be the Hungarian, Georgi Bardos, the reigning World Champion. At the end of his test it was announced that his score was 22. In the end, however, he failed to retain the championship.

Every dressage test is a challenge to both drivers and judges. No matter how experienced the driver or how often the horses have done the

OVERLEAF *An example of the test sheet used by judges for marking.*

FEI DRESSAGE TEST No. 5 (ADVANCED)

COMPETITOR'S NO

....

Time: 10 minutes (for information only)

Errors of course and dismounting of grooms are penalised as follows:—

1st incident . . . . 5 penalty points
2nd incident . . . . 10 penalty points
3rd incident . . . . 15 penalty points
4th incident . . . . Elimination

The Scale of Marks is as follows:—

10. Excellent	4. Insufficient
9. Very good	3. Fairly bad
8. Good	2. Bad
7. Fairly good	1. Very bad
6. Satisfactory	0. Not performed
5. Sufficient	

No.	MOVEMENTS	TO BE JUDGED	MARK 0 – 10	REMARKS
1. A X C	Enter at working trot Halt – salute. Proceed at working trot Track to the right	Driving on a straight line: standing on the bit: transitions to working trot.		
2. M MB	Collected trot 10 metres deviation from side.	Impulsion, regularity and accuracy of figures		
3. PL LI I IS	½ circle to the right 20 metres diameter Extended trot Collected trot ½ circle to the left 20 metres diameter	Impulsion, regularity and accuracy of figures. Transition to extended trot. Transition to collected trot.		
4. EK A	10 metres deviation from side. Turn on centre line	Impulsion, regularity and accuracy of figures.		
5. DX X	Walk on the bit. Halt. Immobile 10 seconds. Rein back 3 metres. Proceed at walk on the bit.	Transition to walk. Straightness, impulsion, regularity. Transition to halt. Immobility. Transition to rein back and to walk.		
6. G C MRXVK K	Collected trot Track to the right Extended trot Working trot	Transition to collected trot. Transition to extended trot. Accuracy, regularity and transition to working trot.		
7. FX X M	Collected trot Reins in one hand and circle to the right 20 metres diameter. Working trot and reins at will.	Accuracy of figures and regularity		

No.	Letter	Movement	To be judged
8.	HSXPF	Extended trot	Transition to extended trot.
	F	Working trot	Regularity, accuracy and transition to working trot.
9.	KX	Collected trot	Accuracy of figures.
	X	Reins in one hand and circle to the left 20 metres diameter	Regularity.
	H	Working trot and reins at will.	
10.	CMSBVFA	Serpentine five loops, 20 metres each turn	Accuracy of figures. Regularity.
	A	Turn on centre line	
11.	D	Collected trot	Accuracy of figures. Regularity.
	L	Circle to the right 15 metre diameters.	Transition to extended trot. Straightness and transition to collected trot. Transition to halt standing straight on the bit.
	LI	Extended trot	
	I	Collected trot and circle to the left 15 metre diameters.	
	G	Halt. Salute.	
12.		Leave arena at working trot	Regularity and freedom (if team, maintenance of pace by all horses)
		Paces	
13.		Impulsion	Moving forward with elasticity of steps. relaxation of the back and engagement. (If equipe, all horses working)
14.		Obedience, lightness	Response to aids, willing and without resistance.
15.		Driver	Use of aids, handling of reins and whip Position on box. Accuracy of figures.
16.		Presentation	Appearance of driver and grooms; cleanliness, fitness, matching and condition of horses, harness and vehicle.
		TOTAL	

Errors of course and dismounting of grooms
To be marked on the President of the Jury's Judging sheet only ....

TOTAL ═══

Signature of Judge ....   Signature of President of the Jury

Prize-giving after the World Championships at Silvasvarad in Hungary in 1984. From left to right: the Swedish team, J.E. Pahlsson (8), C. Pahlsson (12), T. Erickson (15), total 259.5; the Hungarian team, G. Bardos (2), L. Juhasz (1), S. Fulop (E), total 177; the British team, the author (18), M. Flynn (6), G. Bowman (19), total 280.

test, the slightest relaxation of attention can lead to a costly mistake. For judges, who have been mesmerised by a succession of tests on a warm afternoon, it needs a great effort to remain alert enough to spot a mistake instantly and to decide equally instantly whether it is an error of course and ring the bell, or just a movement badly executed.

Having driven many more tests than I have judged, I sympathise with drivers who feel they have been hard done by, but I think they should bear in mind that the judges are doing their best and, very occasionally, they may fail to notice a mistake!

INDEX